GRADE 02

TRUMPET
CORNET & FLUGELHORN

Pieces for Trinity College London
Exams 2019–2022

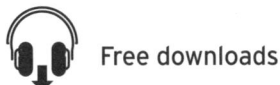 Free downloads

Published by
Trinity College London Press Ltd
trinitycollege.com

Registered in England
Company no. 09726123

© Copyright 2018 Trinity College London Press Ltd
First impression, June 2018

Unauthorised photocopying is illegal
No part of this publication may be copied or reproduced in any
form or by any means without the prior permission of the publisher.

Cover image courtesy of Yamaha Music Europe GmbH
Printed in England by Caligraving Ltd

Group A

The Duke of Gloucester's March

Jeremiah Clarke
(c. 1674-1707)
Arr. Barratt

© Copyright 1996 by Boosey & Hawkes Music Publishers Ltd
Reproduced by permission of Boosey & Hawkes Music Publishers Ltd. from *Bravo! Trumpet* (ISMN 979-0-060-10489-3)

Group A

Acrobats

Alan Bullard
(b. 1947)

© 2002 Spartan Press, Kingussie, PH21 1ER, UK

Group A

Football Game

Christopher Norton
(b. 1953)

© Copyright 1998 by Boosey & Hawkes Music Publishers Ltd
Reproduced by permission of Boosey & Hawkes Music Publishers Ltd
from *Grade by Grade: Trumpet Grade 2* (ISMN 979-0-060-12485-3)

GRADE 02
TRUMPET
CORNET & FLUGELHORN

Pieces for Trinity College London
Exams 2019–2022

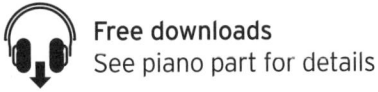

Free downloads
See piano part for details

Published by
Trinity College London Press Ltd
trinitycollege.com

Registered in England
Company no. 09726123

© Copyright 2018 Trinity College London Press Ltd
First impression, June 2018

Unauthorised photocopying is illegal
No part of this publication may be copied or reproduced in any
form or by any means without the prior permission of the publisher.

Cover image courtesy of Yamaha Music Europe GmbH
Printed in England by Caligraving Ltd

Group A

The Duke of Gloucester's March

Jeremiah Clarke
(c. 1674–1707)
Arr. Barratt

Group A

Football Game

Christopher Norton
(b. 1953)

© Copyright 1998 by Boosey & Hawkes Music Publishers Ltd
Reproduced by permission of Boosey & Hawkes Music Publishers Ltd
from *Grade by Grade: Trumpet Grade 2* (ISMN 979-0-060-12485-3)

Group A

Going Crazy

Christopher Wright
(b. 1954)

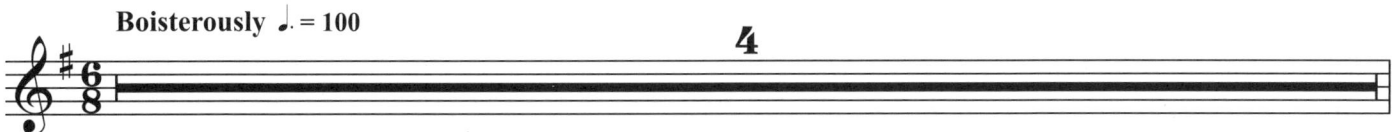

© Copyright C. G. Wright 1995 (from *Going Places*) Omit repeat in the exam.

Group A

Men of Harlech
(duet)

Trad.
Arr. Sparke

O, My Little Augustin

Trad.
Arr. Tomlinson

Group B

Cosmic Ray
from *Astronotes*

Garry Wilkinson
(b. 1958)

Group A

Going Crazy

Christopher Wright
(b. 1954)

8 Omit repeat in the exam. © Copyright C. G. Wright 1995 (from *Going Places*)